To:

From:

MORE

Easy Answers to Life's Hard Questions

BY VIRGINIA REYNOLDS

ILLUSTRATED BY ROBERT ROTH

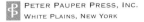

PETER PAUPER PRESS, INC.

WHITE PLAINS, NEW YORK

*For Elizabeth and Heather—
thank you for helping me
find the answers*

Illustrations copyright © 2002
Robert Roth

Designed by Heather Zschock

Text copyright © 2002
Peter Pauper Press, Inc.
202 Mamaroneck Avenue
White Plains, NY 10601
ISBN 0-88088-374-X
Printed in China
7 6 5 4 3

Visit us at www.peterpauper.com

MORE

Easy Answers to Life's Hard Questions

Living in the future
is as much a waste
of time as living in
the past. Don't
squander the precious
moment of now.

The best investment
in your portfolio is
a belief in yourself.

When in doubt,

*immerse yourself
in a bubble bath.*

Listen for the whisper
of your intuition.
The harder you listen,
the louder it will speak.

You cannot know yourself
if you're never alone.
Be still.
Listen to your inner voice.

We need the long, cold winter to fully appreciate the joys of spring.

Friendship doesn't require words. An understanding glance and the touch of a hand can sometimes say far more.

Wherever you can,
sow tolerance and
understanding.

Hard truths are easier to swallow when administered with a dose of humor.

As we need food to
nourish our bodies,
so we need dreams to
nourish our souls.

Those who cannot adapt
to changing conditions
will eventually go the
way of the dinosaurs.

Share your riches,
whatever
they are—
time,
talent,
laughter.

Small physical pleasures—a walk in the woods, a hot bath, a hug—can recharge body and spirit.

The great cathedrals of the world were built one stone at a time...

If you can bend,
you're less
likely to break.

What have you
done today to
make
your corner
of the
world a
better place?

Replace your notion of perfection with one of improvement.

Travel light.
The baggage of the
past can only
hold you back.

Learn to live with chaos.

It can often be beautiful.

Assemble the tiles
of your experience into
the evolving mosaic
that is you.

*Know when to
let go of the urgent
and concentrate on
the important.*

Stop worrying
about where you're
going and focus on
where you are.

Don't waste valuable resources trying to make life fair or lamenting the fact that it isn't.

Find the still, calm center
within yourself and visit
it as often as you can.

Live now. You can't put life on hold.

Honesty, kindness,
generosity—
these are choices,
not inborn traits.

You can learn something
from every person and
every situation, if
you listen carefully
to what they're trying
to teach you.

You can change someone's

day with a kind word.

*Unless you make your
living as a fortune-teller,
don't try to see into
the future.*

*Even when circumstances
are beyond our control,
we can choose how we
react to them.*

If you believe you're
being shortchanged
by time, remember that
you have the same
amount of time each
day as everyone else.

You'll have more time to
concentrate on solving
problems once you accept
that some problems
can't be solved.

Just because somebody is selling something doesn't mean that you need it.

Life is rarely a smooth,
straight road, but the
bumps, twists, and turns
make the journey more
interesting.

It's more difficult to admit you're wrong than to prove you're right.

Home is not an
ornament, a decorator
fabric, or an appliance.
Home is a feeling
in the hearts of the
people who live there.

Wait for a bad mood to pass before making a decision.

Instead of sparring, try dancing.

Everything,
including life,
is temporary.

Simplicity is always elegant, never mundane.

The difference
between quantity and
quality is more than
just a few letters.

Optimism

is its own

reward.

Don't be
afraid to tear
down fences.

Judge behavior,
not people.

Rudeness is never justified.

Action is the antidote to worry.

Common sense

isn't.

You're as rich

as you

believe you are.

Reach out—
you have nothing
to lose but your
solitude.

Laugh at yourself,

and the world will

laugh with you.

Be an early bird.

You'll catch more

than just worms.

Learn to recognize the
early signs of stress.
Take a deep breath.

A listening ear and a few words of comfort can heal a wounded heart.

When offering criticism,
choose your words carefully.
They can be helpful
or hurtful.

A child's laugh is a pure gift.

It's easy to find
fault with yourself
and others—more
challenging to point
out strengths.

Sure, you
can't

do it all.
But you
can do
something.

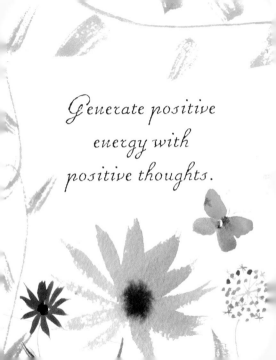

Generate positive
energy with
positive thoughts.

The best outfit you
can wear is a smile.
The second best is
confidence.

You can see obstacles as problems or opportunities.

If you want to score, keep your eye on the goal.

When you find
your passion,
don't test the waters.
Dive right in.

Every day—a fresh canvas!

Paint with bold strokes,

and bright colors.

Live
thoughtfully.

Laugh
often.

Love
generously.